HISTORY IN CAMERA

EAST COAST SHIPPING

A. A. C. HEDGES

D0487327

Shire Publications Ltd.

Copyright © A. A. C. Hedges 1974 and 1989.
First published in 1974. Second Edition 1989.
Number 1 in the History in Camera series. ISBN 0 85263 999 6.

Text typeset on IBM MTSC by Herts Typesetting Services Ltd., Hertford
Printed by C. I. Thomas & Sons (Haverfordwest) Ltd.

All rights reserved. No part of this publication may be reproduced or
transmitted in any form or by any means, electronic or mechanical, including
photocopy, recording, or any information storage and retrieval system,
without permission in writing from the publishers, Shire Publications Ltd.,
Cromwell House, Church Street, Princes Risborough, Aylesbury, Bucks, HP17 9AJ,
U.K.

Cover photograph: 'Lydia Eva' the last of the steam drifters, leading the Tall Ships
down the Yare.

The photograph on the title page shows shipping at the mouth of the Yare
around 1900. The photograph below shows luggers on the Tyne at about the
same time.

Contents

1. *This barque is not aground but trapped in the ice when the Tees was frozen over in 1860. She was registered at Lloyds and given a satisfactory classification, particular attention having been paid to her seaworthiness and operational efficiency. As a result the underwriters assumed her a good risk but she is now in some danger. Lloyds, the world's leading ship classification society, was founded in a coffee house in 1760 and the term 'A1 at Lloyds' was first used in 1775. The present symbol for a first-class ship is '+100 A1'.*

Introduction

This book with its 104 photographs (including a few models, drawings and paintings of particular interest), with its explanatory captions and wide-ranging summary, is more than a chronicle of the ships that sailed the crowded sea lanes of the East Coast between 1860 and 1935. It relates in addition a great deal about the lives of the men who sailed those ships and illustrates the tremendous changes caused by the advent of steam. Steam was instrumental in the decline of great ports such as King's Lynn and Yarmouth and in the rise of others like Grimsby and Teesside. It revolutionised shipbuilding and converted it from a craft industry to one akin to heavy engineering. Much of this era of change is captured in the illustrations, many of which were taken by photographers motivated solely by the desire to obtain an attractive item for their collections. They form a contemporary record of shipping between Blyth and Colchester and are free of the stiffness and formality so often associated with photographs of models, paintings and prints. Devoted to the coaster and inshore vessel, the book is intended to appeal to the general reader but it contains a wealth of information to interest the enthusiast with a passion for ships and the sea.

Britain has always been a trading nation and her emergence as one of the leading industrial powers of the nineteenth century was due in no small part to the strength of her shipping industry. She once had one of the largest fleets in the world, but it has dwindled in the face of competition from Europe and Japan. Nevertheless Britain leads in one respect — her seamen are still the finest in the world — and they continue to enrich a tradition that is centuries old. They have been aggressively supported by ship owners quick to spot a potential outlet and prepared to compete on freight charges. In addition they have always been willing to work the pedestrian but lucrative routes such as those of the East

Coast as well as the more glamorous trans-Atlantic and Far Eastern runs.

The British were among the first to explore the Americas, India, the Far East and Australasia and this has given the history of our shipbuilding a flamboyant air, a sense of *élan*. The stirring deeds of the old sailormen rounding the Horn in their windjammers, their heroism and endurance are all part of this tradition. The hearts of Englishmen, even those who have yet to feel the tang of salt in the air, swell with pride at the recollection of the early British steamships wresting command of the Atlantic from the Americans. Something of this same pride is felt in the *Queen Elizabeth II* even to this day. We are all proud of the achievements of our fighting ships. Every schoolboy knows of Drake's game of bowls on Plymouth Hoe and Nelson's famous message at Trafalgar. No wonder that the Royal Navy which has defended our shores for hundreds of years should hold a special place in the nation's affections.

Yet this book is not about such ships as these. Neither does it concern itself with the clippers and schooners with their intrepid crews, opening up the trade routes of the world. Instead this is the story of the little ships, the colliers, the fishing smacks, the trading vessels of the East Coast. Their tale may lack glamour but romance and drama are there to be found in plenty. The sailormen who manned them were the salt of the earth. Their superb seamanship as well as their ability to endure privation and hardship was unsurpassed. It was, after all, on their skills and enterprise that two profitable industries, shipping and shipbuilding, were developed. Now alas, both are in decline. The importance of these industries has not always been fully recognised. Without them nineteenth- and twentieth-century Britain would have been vastly different.

The physical development and changes in ship design for instance have had an enormous effect on the viability of ports and docks. In the days of sail every seaport on the East Coast boasted a flourishing shipbuilding industry and supported the allied trades associated with it. But as soon as ships became bigger and steel replaced wood, these yards declined. This has affected the lives of thousands of ordinary men and women.

This book then is an attempt in some measure to redress the balance. The story itself is told in the illustrations and their accompanying captions. They are the *raison d'être* of the book. The rest of the text, although wide-ranging, is of necessity the broadest of outlines.

An illustrated history

THE EARLY SHIP

Very early in his development man began to hollow out logs with his flint tools and so built the first primitive canoe. He soon improved on this by covering rude wooden frames with the hides of animals. From then on progress was rapid. The great Mediterranean civilisations of 3000 B.C. produced the sailing ships of the Egyptians and then in succession the rowing galleys of the Cretans, the bireme of the Carthaginians and the carvel-built hull of the Ancient Greeks. The Romans, perhaps the greatest adaptors of all time, realising the potential of sea transport, improved on these designs. Their efficiency was increased by the addition of a second sail, a short mast jutting out over the bow and a paddle-shaped rudder.

A boat with a triangular sail can always be sailed closer to the wind than one fitted with a square sail. The Arabs were the first to discern that. Soon this sail was adopted by most of the Latin peoples and became known in consequence as a lateen. It was not long before it completely superseded the square sail in the Mediterranean. Many ships of this kind visited the East Coast towards the end of the Roman occupation of A.D. 410.

With the withdrawal of the Roman legions trade collapsed and towns began to decline. The East Coast with its sandy beaches and slow-moving rivers running well into the hinterland proved an irresistible attraction to the Vikings. They came in their longboats first as marauding pirates, burning and pillaging as they went, but eventually settling in eastern England. Immediately they began to reopen those trade routes with the Continent established by the Romans. Their ships were clinker-built, shallow-draughted and double-ended with elaborately carved stems and bows. Their steering board was always positioned on the right-hand side of the boat and this side of the vessel came to be known in consequence

as the steerboard or starboard side.

The Normans, who were of Viking extraction, used similar vessels, modified and improved in one or two respects, for the invasion of 1066. Their boats were built with a stern rudder to make navigation easier and were strengthened by the addition of supporting stays. These were, of course, fighting ships and the temporary platforms, called forecastles and sterncastles, erected at the bow and stern were no more than platforms for the archers to fire from. The strengthening of the mast made it possible for a bowman to be positioned aloft. The crow's-nest was now in being.

About 1300 ship design began to incorporate the castles at stem and stern. Oars were dispensed with but the one square sail on a single mast rendered them incapable of sailing against a contrary wind. The largest were of about 300 tons gross.

TRADE AND THE SHIP

In Plantagenet times London was by far the most important port in England but it was dominated by the Hanseatic League, an association of North German merchants. They had achieved this position because the country's economy was dependent upon the export of wool. In consequence the medieval kings were always seeking outlets and were only too pleased to make concessions to the Hans. They carried the wool all over the world.

By 1450 however the English had learned the art of making their own cloth. Woollen exports fell and the entire cloth trade was in the hands of an association of Englishmen known as the Merchant Adventurers Company. They developed the London to Antwerp route but were not interested in opening up trade further afield. This they left to foreigners. By 1485 half of all British exports were carried in ships belonging mainly to the Hanseatic League and the Venetians. There was no English merchant fleet.

Yet a suitable vessel was to hand, for the Portuguese had developed the caravel. This was a ship with three masts, two being square-rigged and the third, the mizzen, being lateen-rigged. With such a ship and the addition of two sails, one set forward beneath the bowsprit and the other a small topsail, Columbus discovered America.

2. (Overpage) *This is the picturesque South Quay in Great Yarmouth in 1860, the hey-day of the port, when dozens of brigs, brigantines and schooners kept the quays and wharves fully occupied. At that time well over a thousand ships were registered in local ownership. By 1903 however the town could lay claim to no more than eighty-six sailing vessels with keels of forty-five feet in length. The days of sail were over.*

3. *Such were the primitive methods of unloading at Port Clarence on Teesside about 1860. Motive power is supplied by the horse on the platform. The beam to which he is harnessed is anchored at the centre, and the chain with the unloading baskets at the end is made fast to the free end of the beam. As the horse is driven forward the chain running over the pulley wheels plucks the loaded hopper from the hold. The swivelling boom enables the load to be easily deposited in the waiting cart.*

In 1551 the European trade in cloth collapsed and merchants were forced to seek new outlets and trade in other commodities such as fish, timber, furs and even slaves. The decline of Antwerp and trouble with the Hanseatic League gave impetus to this need to expand and a group of merchants, the Eastland Company, gained a foothold in the Baltic in 1578. They traded in timber, pitch and ropes, all of which were to prove vital to the shipbuilding industry which flourished along the East Coast for the next 250 years.

A medium-sized ship of just over 200 tons employed in this new trade resembled the galleons of Drake and Hawkins. It was three-masted with additional tops on the fore and main sails and was equipped with armament. Ships of this sort were used against the Spanish Armada and their success heralded the emergence of England as one of the world's greatest trading nations.

COASTING TRADE

From a shipping point of view the value of a cargo is not such an important factor as its bulk. It needs many more ships to transport a thousand pounds' worth of coal than it does to bring back silks and spices to the same value. In 1600 the bulk carriers of Europe in coal, timber and grain were the Dutch who had usurped the role of the Hanseatic League. Eighty-eight per cent of all ships exporting coal from Newcastle were foreign but despite this competition more than half the seamen of England were nevertheless engaged in either the fishing industry or the coal-carrying trade.

The Navigation Act of 1651 was a boon to all East Coast ports. It prohibited foreign ships from bringing into this country cargoes emanating from any country other than their own. This was a grievous blow to the Dutch, but of itself it would not have increased the size of the English fleet by a single hull. In the resultant Anglo-Dutch war of 1652—4, however, so many Dutch ships were captured that the size of the English merchant fleet was doubled. Based on the bulk-carrying trades of timber and coal, East Coast trade now boomed and by the end of the seventeenth century shipbuilders in dozens of small ports were building vessels similar to those captured from the Dutch. Ipswich for instance gained a reputation for the building of large colliers. Later the bulk of this trade moved farther up the East Coast and by the middle of the eighteenth century places such as Whitby and Sunderland were thriving shipbuilding centres. So great was this expansion that supplies of English oak became scarce and timber was imported from the Baltic to replace it. Other materials needed in shipbuilding, flax for the sails, pitch and tar for water-proofing and hemp for the ropes, were also imported and so the Baltic trade flourished on the back of the home shipbuilding industry.

English shipping became concentrated on the East Coast and was engaged in either the coastal or European trades. These bulk carriers, unlike the modern tramp steamers, did not voyage round the world picking up cargoes en route, but concentrated on one commodity and worked one route. It was customary however for many timber ships to transfer in the winter months to the lucrative wine trade with France.

The end of the eighteenth century and the whole of the nineteenth witnessed a rapid expansion of English shipping but America was now the growing market absorbing all the manufactured articles resulting from the industrial revolution. The Western ports were now much more strategically placed for

4. *Elaborate carvings and large figureheads were introduced to decorate huge merchant vessels and warships from 1600. A highly decorated stern and galleries with rich side carvings were the order of the day. Over the next two hundred years superstructures were reduced until even forecastle and poop were concealed by a continuous sheer line. In the last days of sail, ships were decorated with only simple figureheads and a scroll or two on the stern.*

5. *Middlesbrough* (below) *was one of those new ports which became established largely as a result of the Industrial Revolution. In 1801 it consisted of only a few farmhouses and had a total population of twenty-five. In 1830 the Stockton and Darlington railway was extended to Middlesbrough and a port was established to facilitate the shipment of coal. By now the population had soared to 5,709. The first blast furnaces were erected in 1850 and Teesside soon became a thriving iron centre.*

handling this business and gradually wrested the initiative from the ports in the East. Moreover as trade became world-wide it was more economic to carry it in larger ships. Many ports which were once thriving and important now discovered that they were unable to take these larger ships and the importance of the East Coast began to wane.

Fewer men were now employed in shipbuilding and the entire economic growth of the East Coast began to slow down.

THE CHANGING SHIP

Early merchantmen, especially if trading far from home waters, normally carried sufficient armament to protect themselves against pirates and corsairs. In the seventeenth century this was still true of vessels engaged in the Far Eastern trade but soon ships designed

6. *The 'Tranquillity' SH9, built in Scarborough in 1866 and pictured here in that self-same port a few years later, was fifty-nine feet long and thirty-nine tons register. She is dandy-rigged, that is fitted with a gaff mainsail and a mizzen. The harbour, with its two basins enclosed by two piers, is dry at low tide. At high water it is accessible to vessels drawing up to twelve feet and is still much favoured by inshore fishing boats. It has been controlled by Harbour Commissioners since 1843.*

solely for the carrying of cargo were introduced into the coasting trade.

These two-masted vessels, known as brigs, were square-rigged on both masts except for a fore and aft spanker and they were so efficient that they ousted all other craft from the coal-carrying trade, becoming the most common of all cargo-carrying coasters. They were utilitarian vessels with no figureheads or elaborately decorated sterns, but magnificent sea boats quite capable of sailing the oceans of the world.

Until the end of the eighteenth century it was normal practice to describe ships by the shape of their hulls. Later it was the masts and rigging that became the distinguishing factors. This is understandable for by 1800 the three-masted ship was carrying over three times the amount of sail that the Portuguese caravel had done 250 years earlier. The warship *Royal Sovereign* built in 1637 had shown the way. By having a fourth set of sails on the main foremast she encouraged shipbuilders to introduce additional canvas to merchantmen. Extensions to the mainsail and topsail booms on the fore and main mast were obvious ways of increasing the sail area but the introduction of the jib in 1720 revolutionised design.

This triangular sail, spread between the bowsprit and the foremast, had been used on single-masted ships since the sixteenth century and as soon as it was fitted to larger vessels it increased the merchantman's ability to make progress against a head wind. This was a particularly valuable asset to a ship engaged in the coastal trade of the North Sea with its strong prevailing winds and conflicting tides. Then before 1800 a flying jib was introduced. This was followed by other triangular sails spread on the ropes or stays designed to support the mast. All of these were of the greatest assistance in tacking against adverse conditions. At about the same time the spanker gaff, held out at an angle from the mizzen, began to oust the lateen yard and this made it possible for yacht-like sails to be used in favourable winds.

So revolutionary and so effective were these improvements that by 1900 the two-masted brig was supreme and employed not only in the European trade but also in the Atlantic. Basically however the sailing ship had not changed for three hundred years. It had been modified and perfected to meet the changing requirements of war and peace and it seemed that no task was beyond it. Just over the horizon however lay the steamship and in a short space of time she was to drive the sailing ships from the seas and oceans of the world.

FISHING AND THE DRIFTER

Fish were an important item in the nation's diet from the earliest times but because of the difficulties of transportation (the roads were poor and the railways non-existent) the river and fresh-water fisheries were the first to be developed. Sea fishing was limited in consequence to those fish which could be effectively dried and then marketed. Chief of these was the herring. By the middle of the thirteenth century it had become a favourite food with people in all walks of life. Henry III even purchased them to distribute as alms and the monasteries bought large quantities as part of their Lenten observance. In 1427 the herring changed its habits. It deserted the Baltic for the North Sea and gave the impetus to develop and improve our sea fisheries. The Dutch however had been quick to seize the opportunity and were soon in a dominating position due not only to the size of their fleets but also to their method of curing at sea. This process was kept a closely guarded secret for well over a hundred years. The ships, or busses, in which they were caught and cured were similar to the small trading craft of that period. They were bluff in the bow with neither forecastle nor aftercastle. They sported one heavy mast amidships carrying a huge square sail as well as a bowsprit. Later, as ship design improved, they followed the trend set by the larger merchantmen and introduced both foremast and mizzen.

A further improvement came with the invention of a plain spar called a vargord. This extended the weather leech of the square sail and made it possible to dispense with the bowline and bowsprit and this led to the introduction of the lugsail. So successful was this new rig that by 1850 the buss had been completely replaced by the herring lugger. Broadly speaking this period coincided with the Napoleonic Wars and as a result of the tight blockade of Europe maintained by the Allies the Dutch lost and never regained their trading and fishing monopolies.

Between 1840 and 1870 the lugger gradually changed to a two-masted rig and then to a dandy rig. The Scots were now a force to be reckoned with as they followed the herring all down the East Coast, landing their catch at the nearest and most convenient port. They, as much as the extensive fishing grounds

7. (Opposite) *In the nineteenth century thousands of seamen owed their lives to the invention of the rocket life-saving apparatus incorporating the breeches buoy which was invented by Captain W. G. Manby. This picture depicts the epic rescue on 2nd April 1866 when the apparatus was used for the very first time by a volunteer life brigade, a unit from South Shields. The Sunderland schooner 'Tenterden' had gone aground just off the coast in atrocious weather but the crew of seven, the master, his wife and baby daughter were all saved.*

8. *One hundred years ago shipbuilding was carried out in such yards as this all round the coast. They boasted no machinery — except a crude lathe — all the work being done with hand tools. A capstan worked by a horse would suffice for hauling out and a block and tackle fixed to a handy spar was sufficient to swing the largest piece of timber into position. Sawyers worked in the saw pit in the foreground of the photograph (one on top and one down below) cutting out the strakes from the huge logs brought to the yard by horse-drawn drugs. The yard shown here is Hewitts of Great Yarmouth.*

off Smith's Knoll and the elaborate gutting and curing facilities ashore, were instrumental in making Yarmouth the premier herring port in the world.

At the turn of the century sail gradually gave way to steam and in 1913 no fewer than 1,163 steam drifters were fishing from Yarmouth alone. They caught between them nearly two and a half million hundredweight of fish, or well over 800,000 cran, of which eighty per cent were exported. But two world wars, the absence of the herring from its familiar haunts and over-fishing have caused the collapse of the East Coast herring industry and now not a single drifter fishes from Yarmouth.

Trawling for fish was introduced to the East Coast by men from Brixham and Barking about 1840. They used beam trawls and in order to cope with the additional weight introduced a specially adapted cutter-rigged smack to do the job. The mainsail was enlarged, the length of the hull increased and a small mizzen stepped abaft the stern post. The mizzen sail was then fitted with a gaff like the mainsail. Vessels adapted in this way are often described as 'ketch-rigged'. These ketches were both fast and seaworthy and soon became established in all the East Coast ports from Hull to the Nore Sandbank. The old two-masted luggers were quite unable to compete and by 1880 most of them had been rigged for gaff sails and many drifters also tried their hands at trawling.

9. *The first dockyard on Teesside was erected in Middlesbrough in 1842 largely as a result of the country's insatiable appetite for coal and the booming coastal collier trade. But as early as 1866, the date on this engraving, Middlesbrough had become the centre of the iron ore industry. The stone was mined in the nearby Cleveland Hills. A proportion of the brigs in the background would be loaded with iron ore, for in 1870 one third of a million tons was exported to Europe and the same amount carried down the English coast.*

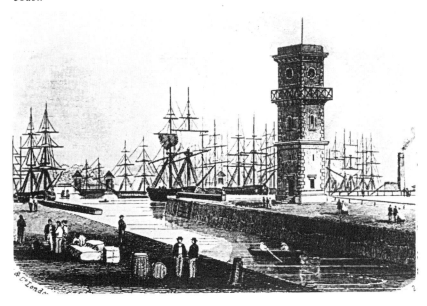

The advent of Hewett's Short Blue Fleet, based at Barking and then at Gorleston, completely revolutionised fishing in the North Sea. Not only did they fish in fleets in the charge of an admiral but they also fished as directed. They were usually at sea for six to eight weeks. Every day their catches were ferried across to the carrier in open boats. The carrier was often a steam auxiliary which, when laden, made full speed to catch the market at Billingsgate. This operation, known as trunking, from the boxes or trunks into which the fish were packed aboard the smacks, was particularly hazardous. But fishermen's lives were cheap and the Londoner's insatiable appetite for fresh fish had to be satisfied.

Steam vessels were used for trawling almost by chance. The owner of the tug *Messenger* from Hull, unable to obtain towing commissions, noticed that on calm days the smacks often had their trawls down when being towed to the fishing grounds. Why not let his tug tow the trawl without the assistance of the smack? He successfully put his theory to the test in 1885 and the heyday of the sailing trawler was over.

In the next few years many steam trawlers were built and ports such as Grimsby, Hull and Lowestoft came into their own by providing facilities for these larger ships. They were assisted by the railway companies too who in some instances owned the wharves and docks. But in any event they were not slow to recognise the advantages that would accrue from these new developments and co-operated in every way.

Inevitably as the size of the ships and the efficiency of their gear and methods increased so their catches soared. Soon the North Sea was over-fished and catches decreased alarmingly. Local fleets have dwindled and trawlers are now forced to go much farther afield — to Iceland and the Faroes — in search of their catches. As a result it has now become imperative that vessels should be able to stay at sea for longer periods without causing undue strain on their crews. Since the Second World War more heed has been paid to working conditions and this, along with the high price of coal, has accelerated the swing from steam to diesel.

INSHORE CRAFT

Apart from these deep-sea fishing vessels there is a particular inshore boat associated with each part of the coast which has developed to suit local conditions. The cobles of Yorkshire and Northumberland, the Cromer crab boats, the yawls of Southwold, the oyster catchers of Colchester and the Yarmouth shrimpers are all typical.

THE SEAMAN'S LOT

Throughout the seventeenth and eighteenth centuries the British were fighting the Dutch and the French. In both centuries much of the action took place on the high seas and the merchant seaman was in the thick of it. There was no escape even for those engaged in the East Coast trade. Every sail threatened a potential enemy, a privateer perhaps, and the seaman was never safe until he reached port. Even then he had to be on his guard, for as usual the Navy was short of men and the press gangs were at work. If he were seized it was 'goodbye' to wife and family for many a long day.

Life in the Merchant Navy was not a bed of roses. There was much that was wrong with the service. Many ships were

10. *This chain ferry is about to disembark its passengers, including a horse and cart, on the south side of the river Blyth. Until the middle of the nineteenth century the channel and harbour were in their natural state and the river dried out at low water. Now the bed of the river has been blasted out and deep water quays have been constructed so that 12,000 ton ships have no difficulty in entering Blyth. Modern coaling staithes with their electric belt conveyors and equipment designed to minimise breakage made it the country's premier coaling port.*

unseaworthy, officers were often incompetent and had but a rudimentary knowledge of navigation. Some captains too were prepared to risk the loss of their crews in order to get ships to port on time and earn the gratitude of the owners. Many ships were grossly overloaded. It is no wonder that between 1866 and 1875 nearly ten thousand ships, excluding fishing vessels, were wrecked. The great majority of these were collier brigs on their way to and from the Tyne.

Seamen could refuse to sail in any ship they considered unseaworthy but the risk of ending up in gaol for doing so was great enough to deter the majority from complaining. The public conscience however, becoming more and more uneasy at this reckless waste of lives, spurred successive governments to remedy these abuses. Even the long-established crimping system was controlled and those keepers of unsavoury boarding houses, who enticed seamen with full pockets into their establishments with the lure of strong drink and fast women, found the going harder. Missionary societies such as the Mission to Seamen and the British Sailors' Society also helped a great deal by re-educating the men.

Despite all these abuses and the incompetence and excesses of the few, the average coasting skipper was a man to be greatly admired. He had learned his trade the hard way, went to sea as a boy and worked his way up by his own efforts to the command of a brig. This was no sinecure for it should be remembered that the first chart of the North Sea was not drawn until 1847 and the information it conveyed, even to those able to read it, was incomplete and unreliable. The depths of banks and shoals still had to be ascertained by leads armed with tallow and these readings plus the experience of years enabled these magnificent seamen to pinpoint their position. Even such intangible things as the colour of the water and the run of the tides were taken into account.

The North Sea with its area of 152,000 square miles, its huge seas, conflicting tides and sudden variations in weather, is the most treacherous sea in the world. It was once the busiest and with ships sailing from the Scandinavian ports, collier brigs travelling from the Tyne to the Thames and large fleets of fishing vessels all jockeying for sea room, collisions were inevitable. Our debt to these humble, often illiterate men, is enormous.

MAKING THE SEA LANES SAFE

Public opinion now demanded that these East Coast sea lanes be made safe. Trinity House, incorporated in 1566, had been made

11. *In the days of sail there was little protection from the elements between the Thames and the Humber. In bad weather hundreds of collier brigs, ketches, topsail schooners and spritsail barges would ride out the gale in Yarmouth Roads. This anchorage, seen here on a fine summer day in 1870, is some six miles long and a mile wide with a depth of between five and twelve fathoms. The sea bed of sand, mud and stones makes firm holding ground.*

12. *In 1870 there was plenty of work for shipwrights and other tradesmen; but a hardy race of men, perhaps lacking the patience and skill to follow a craft, gained a livelihood from salvage. Anchors were particularly valuable, regularly fished for and brought to an anchor ground like the one displayed here. A skipper losing his anchor in a gale would know where to come for a replacement. When he had set sail the beachmen would then fish or 'swipe' for the original anchor. Later it was customary for the anchors to be purchased by H. M. Customs at half-a-crown per hundredweight.*

responsible for the erection of the first lighthouse at Lowestoft in 1609 but the difficulties of erecting substantial edifices on the sandy shores of the East Coast had inhibited them from further building. Some had been erected privately. Coverage was uneven and it was not until 1836 that Trinity House was able to buy out the private owners and establish a coherent system of powerful warning lights.

Next, buoys to mark the extent of the shoals and the limits of the sandbanks were introduced. The most intricate channel could now be safely negotiated. These aids to navigation, plus the fact that the steamship was intrinsically safer than the sailing vessel, brought about a substantial reduction in the number of shipwrecks. Nevertheless there were more than enough to ensure that the homes for shipwrecked seamen were never empty for long. Even the warnings of impending gales transmitted over the newly established telegraphic stations by the Board of Trade could not prevent many tragedies.

The rescue of men at sea remained largely the preserve of the companies of beachmen established round the coast. Insensible to danger these brave men would put out to sea in their fast open yawls to save the lives of others or to rescue valuable cargo. They lived by salvage. Theirs was a hard, exacting, dangerous life and many a man was washed overboard and lost forever.

There was enough to do in all conscience for in one December gale, in 1863, no fewer than twenty ships from Yarmouth alone were wrecked and their crews of 145 men were all drowned. This work of rescue was continued by the Volunteer Lifeboats operating on a local basis and then by the Shipwreck Institutes and the Royal National Lifeboat Institution established in 1824.

The sailing and pulling lifeboats of those days were far removed from the self-righting craft of today with their powerful engines but the Norfolk and Suffolk type designed by Lionel Lukin and built by James Beeching was perhaps the most successful lifeboat ever launched.

H.M. Coastguards, although recruited originally to combat the smuggler, have also developed into a life-saving organisation. Apart from maintaining an effective look-out system the Coastguards also control the rocket life-saving apparatus with the breeches buoy originally introduced by Captain W. G. Manby.

Although conditions at sea have changed for the better men's lives are occasionally at risk and then these well tried and trusted organisations swing smoothly into action.

THE AGE OF STEAM

The year 1870 was a turning point in the history of British shipping. In that year registered sailing tonnage reached a peak of over 4½ million tons compared with the steamers' total of 901,000 tons, but from then on sail steadily declined whilst the tonnage of steamships increased.

The success of the steamship was due in a large measure to the development of the compound engine until it was capable of driving four pistons. Consequently fuel consumption was reduced and more space reserved for cargo.

Steam vessels were originally propelled by paddles but the introduction of the screw propeller produced a dramatic increase in efficiency. Twin screws were introduced about 1888 and the installation of fast-running machines which were more compact and used even less fuel freed further cargo space. Technical progress continued and in 1894 the turbine engine invented by Sir Charles Parsons was successfully fitted to the first East Coast cargo ships.

Another important development was the introduction of the

iron hull. This was much lighter and made possible the building of larger ships. As far as the East Coast was concerned this had two major effects. Firstly a number of ports like King's Lynn, Wells and Yarmouth had few berths capable of accommodating these new vessels and their importance declined as trade was diverted elsewhere. Secondly the old ways of building ships were over. Now size and scale were of first importance and it was necessary to work close to the raw materials.

A new industry was established centred on the Tyne and shipbuilding declined in all the East Coast ports. Even at Ipswich, once the most thriving centre of all, no more ships were built.

In the First World War the merchant fleet, especially East Coast shipping, suffered severely and only a small proportion of the lost tonnage was ever replaced. Then came the slump and the economic crisis of 1931. Tramp steamers and coasting vessels were laid up in every river estuary around the coast. The decline in the export of coal, once the staple cargo of the East Coast ships, was a disaster particularly as there was no other bulk cargo to replace it. Between 1930 and 1938 the export of coal, almost all of it carried in East Coast ships, declined by over forty million tons per annum.

The country's appetite for oil grew and grew, but the British tanker fleet was small and many of the ships seen in our ports at that time were chartered by the petroleum companies from their Norwegian owners. A reluctance to install the more economical diesel engines also added to the general malaise and by 1932 the industry was in such distress that the traditional free trade policy was abandoned and shipping was protected by a tariff. In 1935 the government went even further and decided to subsidise charter rates. It was the end of an era in British shipping.

13. (Opposite) *The Lowestoft smack 'Early Blossom' LT 16, like most of her kind, had a registered tonnage of forty-five tons and a length overall of about seventy-five feet. She was built at Galmpton, Devon, in 1908. Compared with trawlers with elliptical sterns built in Lowestoft in the 1870s by Fuller Bros. Ltd. she was cheaper to build, probably costing about £700, and cheaper to maintain. She would be at sea from seven to ten days. Generally speaking Lowestoft smacks preferred to fish singly rather than in fleets and used the grounds nearer home.*

14. (Opposite) *A century ago wrecks and collisions at sea were commonplace and the appalling loss of life which resulted was as heavy as on today's roads. This wreck chart of 1873 showing the vessels lost off our shores in a single year is almost unbelievable. But one look at a modern sea chart shows that the major hazards lay across the busiest sea lane of the time — the direct route from the Tyne to London. It is perhaps not surprising then that a large proportion of the wrecks occurred off the East Coast with its shifting and treacherous sandbanks and narrow channels.*

15. *After 1872 the first Scarborough yawls began to appear rigged with a foresail, fore and aft mainsail with a bonnet and mizzen. As a result they were easier to handle under sail and when drifting for herring were capable of handling 120 nets, each sixty yards long and twelve yards in depth. One of the smaller 'calf' cobles, two of which were carried on deck, lies alongside. These small vessels were used either for line fishing or for catching small herring as bait. Larger cobles with lugsails complete the picture taken about 1898.*

16. *During the 1880s the popularity of the lugsail began to wane and on the larger fishing vessels they were replaced by gaff sails. The drifter 'Five Sisters', built in 1875 for C. W. Basey, is like most Yarmouth boats in that her mast is still stepped in a tabernacle as the lugsail had been. This produced a much less lofty sail plan than in boats whose design was derived from the cutter.*

17. (Below) *Among this forest of masts the spritsail on the farther bank is particularly prominent on account of her blunt bows and transom stern. Spritsails were flat-bottomed and had lee boards.*

18. (Opposite) *This seaman in Ipswich about 1880 typifies the breed who saw service in the brigs employed in the bulk carrying trade. He probably went to sea as a cabin boy and then after a spell as able seaman was promoted to cook. The cook often took the Master's watch and with this experience he was spurred on to gain a command for himself.*

19. (Below) *A bluff-bowed brigantine, probably from the Tyne, settles happily alongside two yawls in Scarborough harbour about 1880. The high conical capstan, or iron horse, just forward of the mizzen mast on the yawl to the left of the picture is an important feature. It was this capstan which, with the help of four men tramping round it for hour after hour, hauled in the nets. These were cleared at sea and the herring shovelled down a hatch on deck known as the well. All the rigging was of hemp, hence the large blocks.*

20. (Top right) *The skipper of this smack expected, in 1882, a commission on the value of his catch to supplement his weekly wage. This would be one shilling in the pound on the first £100 plus four shillings in the pound on the next £50. If the catch was worth more than that he would receive a fifth of the total. The six man crew were all paid in this way — a fixed wage plus commission — but the sixth hand could only hope for a bonus of two pence in the pound to add to his weekly wage of eight shillings.*

21. (Lower right) *Fish carriers like this vessel, photographed at Yarmouth as early as 1880, were an integral part of fishing as practised by the great fleets of East Coast smacks. After every haul the fish were gutted, washed and sorted into wooden boxes known as trunks and these, no matter how atrocious the weather, were ferried across to the carrier in a small but beamy open rowing boat. Once she was fully laden, the carrier sped off for Billingsgate leaving the smacks to continue fishing until her return.*

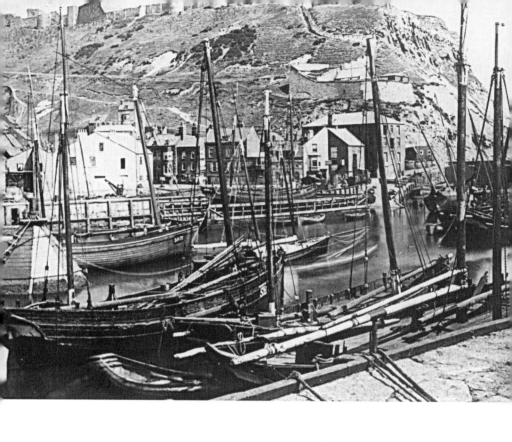

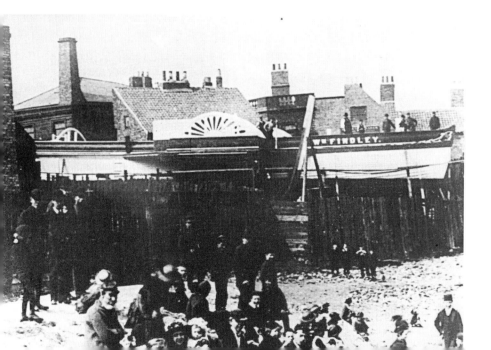

22. (Top left)'*Meliora*' *SH71, in the background of this photograph, taken in Scarborough about 1880, is a typical Scarborough yawl. The design was derived from that of the beach yawls of the Norfolk coast, but the Yorkshiremen had greater depth. It was introduced about 1833 to replace the larger and much more expensive 'five-man' boats. 'Meliora' still has her original rig here of a dipping lug foresail with a standing lug mizzen and jib.*

23. (Lower left) *The 'William Findley'. Throughout the nineteenth century, as iron replaced wood and steam superseded sail, shipbuilding became more of an assembly industry closely related to heavy engineering. The scattered yards along the Tyne were later in developing than those on Wearside but by 1884, the date of this photograph, the seeds had been sown. This is the yard of Wouldhave and Johnson of Low Lights, North Shields, and shows a clinker-built paddle steamer on the stocks.*

24. (Above) *A strange rig for a Yarmouth smack in about 1885 but sensible nevertheless. The mizzen mast has to be stepped forward sufficiently to permit free movement of the tiller (the wheel was not yet in use) but if it is moved any further forward then the size of the mainsail will have to be reduced for the mainmast is already stepped well forward cramping the foresail in the process. The sail on the mizzen is increased in area by stretching it on a pole. The mainsail is free footed like so many dandy-rigged vessels.*

25. (Top left) *No visit to the seaside in Victorian days was complete without a shrimp tea and this fleet of shrimpers is returning on the morning tide in the summer of 1886 so that their catch can be on sale at tea-time. The season began very early in the Spring and continued until mid-October. Until the end of June the brown shrimp was considered the most delicious but after this the pink shrimp, trawled in deep water, was preferred.*

26. (Lower left) *Neither was a holiday complete without a trip round the harbour; as true in 1890 as it is now, as this photograph from Scarborough shows. While the position of the couple balancing on the gangplank supported on two wheels seems a little precarious, that of the group of would-be voyagers in the cart seems positively hazardous. The picture illustrates the suitability of cobles for working off beaches and 'Propriety' in the foreground is one of the double-ended type popular in Scarborough by 1870.*

27. (Below) *Not only sailing vessels but steamers also were at risk in the North Sea at the turn of the century. Few disasters had such dire financial consequences for those ashore as that of the 'Wick Bay' on 23rd December 1889. She was an iron steamer of 1,193 tons which ran aground and broke her back in the Wash with a cargo from Baltimore of cattle feed and maize worth £50,000. King's Lynn Corporation were forced to raise a loan of £16,688 at three per cent to clear the channel.*

28. (Below) *These Fifies or keel boats, photographed about 1905, were popular with the Scots. They are carvel built and double-ended but, unlike the Zulu, the stern post is vertical. When the foremast, which has no shrouds, is lowered it rests in a crutch positioned to the starboard of the mizzen mast. This mast is about two-thirds of the size of the foremast and rakes forward. The bumkin to which the standing lug on the mizzen is sheeted is run out specifically for the purpose. Fifies were normally painted black with a little white at the bow.*

29. (Top right) *Mechanised methods in the making of ropes were unknown in the hey-day of sail. In this photograph of a rope walk, dating from about 1890, the spinners have received the dressed hemp from the dressers and are walking backwards releasing the hemp as they go. They would first have made fast a strand or two upon the 'wheel-head'. Meanwhile a boy is slowly turning this wheel to bind the twine together. On the return journey the spinner uses a grooved conical-shaped wooden 'top' which binds the individual threads into a single twine.*

30. (Lower right) *When the opportunity arose, the nineteenth-century seaman sought self-expression with the tools and materials near at hand — a penknife, a marlinspike and odd pieces of scrap timber. The things he produced, simple and unsophisticated, had an inherent charm and sincerity. Sometimes, instead of wood, he carved dried salt beef which was as hard as wood and almost indistinguishable from it, especially when painted. Many instances have been known after long enforced spells at sea for models to be dismantled, soaked and consigned to the pot.*

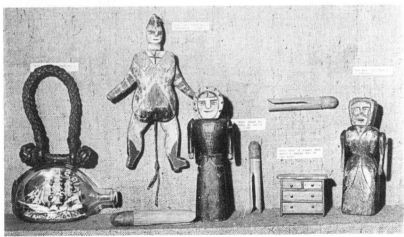

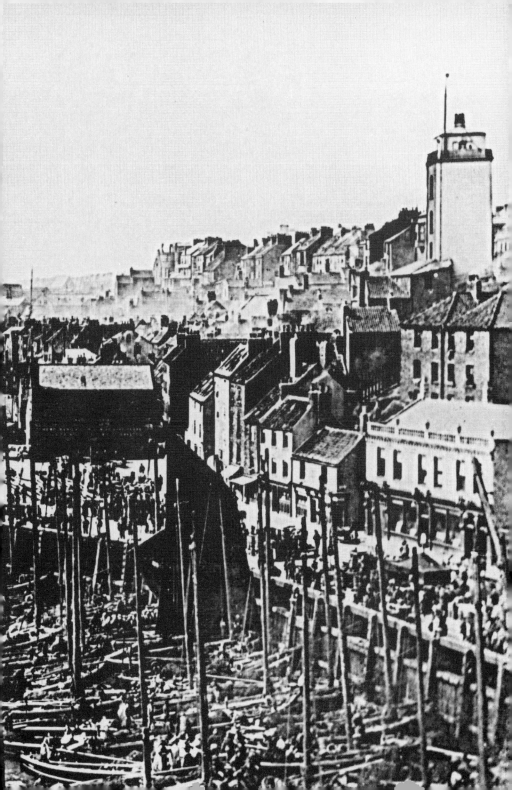

31. This is the port of Ipswich about 1890. The Vikings discovered a port
there in 991 but the modern port dates from 1805 when power was vested in
the River Commission. By 1830 Ipswich was competing for bulk cargoes with
Yarmouth and Lynn and was shipping to London 80,000 quarters of malt
annually. Facilities on the Orwell were further improved in 1843 by the
building of the largest wet dock in Britain. The water surface of thirty-two
acres exceeded that of Hull by nine and London by three acres. Vessels of
over a thousand tons could now berth there.

32. (Over page) These Northumberland cobles lying alongside larger ships at
the Low Lights, North Shields, were clinker-built and rigged with a single lofty
mast raked aft which carried a lugsail and a jib. They were excellent sea boats
and carried a large amount of sail for their size. They were able to do so
because of the length and design of their rudders which projected some four
feet below the boat and acted as a subsidiary keel. In this photograph, dating
from about 1890, a number of these rudders have been unshipped and left
lying athwart the stern.

33. *Until 1822, when Robert Hamblin of King's Lynn suggested that a floating light be installed at the Nore to assist vessels entering the Thames, the mariner had no marks once out of sight of land to help him negotiate the treacherous shoals of the East Coast. This was the forerunner of familiar red-hulled vessels like the 'Roaring Middle'.*

34. (Below) *The paddle tug 'United Service', photographed here about 1890 with three Scots fishing vessels in tow, was a dual purpose vessel. In summer she was a familiar sight to holidaymakers on the Norfolk coast. Then she was used as a pleasure steamer for trips in the North Sea. When winter came she was stripped of her holiday gear and she reverted to the more humdrum task of towing vessels in and out of harbour.*

35. (Top left) *This is the Yorkshire mule 'Mizpah', built in Filey in 1890, a few years after her launching. Boats of her type were called mules because the forward part resembled the coble whilst the after part was derived from the yawl. The whaler-like stern which replaced the flat transom of the coble enabled her to sail with safety with a following sea — a difficult task for a coble. They were more difficult to beach than cobles and favoured enclosed harbours. She was twenty-six feet long and four tons net.*

36. (Lower left) *The Lowestoft shrimper 395LT puts to sea in 1892 with the aid of a pair of oars worked in double thole pins. The mainsail has two reef pendants rove. The small jacky topsail raked sharply forward and the transom stern are distinctive features. The beam trawl is clearly shown on the port side.*

37. (Right) *The paddle tug 'Tom Perry' is pictured here about 1892 with two Scots sailing drifters from Banff and Kirkcaldy in tow. She was built on the Tyne in 1879, and designed as a light draught tug intended for salvage work as much as for general harbour towage. She played an important part in the ill-fated attempts to rescue the fully-rigged ship 'Soudan' of Liverpool when she was aground on the Cross Sands in 1896 as well as salvaging the Russian timber ship 'Antares' in 1900. She was almost the same size and tonnage as the 'William Findley' (page 34).*

38. *A bizarre contrast this, dating from 1896. The crowd has assembled on Yarmouth's picturesque South Quay not to see the collier brigs unloading but to watch the procession of Barnum and Bailey's circus. The foremost brig 'Messenger' was regularly employed in the Tyne coal trade and like other colliers introduced into service in the late nineteenth century is fitted with a bentinck boom on the forecourse. The tallest mill ever built in England, Press High Mill, measuring 120 feet from toe to cap, can be seen in the background.*

39. (Above) *The brigantine photographed lying alongside the Custom House at Ipswich in about 1893 is a reminder that there was a regular customs service on the East Coast even in Norman times. In the middle ages it was usual for the Crown to 'farm out' the customs to the highest bidder. He for his part exacted as much as he could from those liable in order to make his operation a profitable one. This led to abuses and in 1671 Charles II made the service a fully professional one as it has remained to this day.*

40. (Top right) *Sometimes in the 1890s skippers of sailing vessels of all types found it expedient to unload their cargoes on to open beaches rather than attempt to enter a difficult harbour in the face of adverse weather conditions. Instead they found a safe anchorage and then off-loaded their cargo, usually coal or fish, into baskets ferried out to them in open boats with a good carrying capacity. The baskets were then taken up the beach to a waiting cart by two men who linked arms and balanced them on their shoulders.*

41. (Lower right) *An interested spectator watches from the stern of a laid-up smack as the brig unloads her cargo of timber from the Baltic in the port of Yarmouth about 1897. Unlike the brig astern she is unloading not onto the quayside but directly into a wherry moored alongside. She in her turn will carry it up the Yare — almost certainly to Norwich. The number and variety of vessels moored on the opposite bank — a smack, a barge, several brigs and two paddle tugs — illustrates how important this port once was.*

42. (Right) *Lugger skipper James 'Gilbert' George, Master of the sailing drifter 'Archer', poses in 1899 with his wife by his side and his grand-daughter on his knee. There are still identical cottages in the village of Winterton. The next voyage seems far from his thoughts as he sits there in his own back garden with the fruits of his labours ashore — a crop of parsnips — at his feet. Like most fishermen of the time he preferred dried fish to fresh fish and just under the wall tie to the right of the kitchen door he has hung out to dry two herring on their speet.*

43. (Below) *When Hewett and Co of Barking transferred their fleet of smacks, known as the Short Blue, to Gorleston in 1854 they revolutionised fishing in the North Sea. At the height of its prosperity the company owned two hundred vessels and its trawling fleet was the largest in the country. It also established dry docks, yards, sailmakers' lofts and carpenters' shops to maintain it. Throughout the 1900s the company experienced fierce competition from the newly established steam trawling fleets from Hull and Grimsby. The end came in 1902. This photograph shows some of the ships laid up at Gorleston where the militia encamped in 1897.*

44. (Below) *On 26th March 1898 the barque 'Diamant' went aground at Tynemouth and the crew of eight were rescued by rocket apparatus. Originally this consisted of a metal shot with a light line attached which was fired from a mortar on the beach to the ship in the breakers. This line, and the thicker one tied to it and rove through a block with a cradle attached, was pulled inboard. One end was made fast to the mast and the other secured on shore. The cradle could now be pulled to and fro until all were saved.*

45. (Right) *By the middle of the eighteenth century Sunderland was a well-known seaport, coal-mining town and important shipbuilding centre. But the shipyards and industries were small in scale and concentrated in the old town of Sunderland. Farther up the Wear the shores were sandy, marshy and undeveloped. A hundred and fifty years later, when this photograph was taken, wet docks had been established, coaling points built and shipyards had sprung up all along the estuary.*

46. (Top left) *The photographer himself is caught recording the arrival of this smack with her house flag flying proudly at the foremast, towed into Yarmouth harbour by one of the port's many paddle tugs, about 1898. In all probability she has been away for six weeks and her owners will expect her to have made around £170 for the trip. They will have seen her arrival in the roads from their lofty watch-tower on the sea front.*

47. (Lower left) *The earliest steam drifters were greeted with derision when they first joined the fishing fleets about 1901. Despite this initial scepticism the steamer was soon to prove that she was as adept at drift net fishing as at trawling and in a few years the sailing drifter was obsolete. Here is one of the earliest of all steam drifters, the 'Resolute' of Leith and later owned at Lowestoft, leading a mixed fleet of sailing and steam drifters across the bar one windy day a few years later. A sizeable crowd has gathered on Gorleston Pier to watch them come in.*

48. (Lower right) *The iron paddle tug 'Marie' of King's Lynn negotiating the channel at Wells about 1900 with a Dutch leeboard barge in tow. All down the East Coast these tugs were used to tow sailing vessels out of harbour, the maximum tow permitted being five smacks. Many of these twin-funnelled tugs were built at North Shields, the most famous being 'Powerful' in 1856.*

49. *King's Lynn was an important port for well over a thousand years and has always been noted for its trade in linseed cake for cattle brought in by Russian and German vessels such as this. They then reloaded with coal for the journey home. About 1901, the probable date of this picture, there was also a brisk business in timber.*

50. *This three-masted barque has just unloaded her cargo of 1,000 tons of wheat from Australia at J. J. Colman's wharf at Yarmouth. The wheat was conveyed in bags which have been carried into the warehouse in the background. This had a capacity of 5,000 tons and was intended for the storage of rice. A Thames sailing barge lies astern and a wherry, with her mast lowered to enable her to shoot the bridge, is up for'ard. The date is 1900.*

51. *By 1901 steam had ousted sail in Grimsby. The greater reliability of these modern ships made it possible for them to return to port with each catch. Most had no need of the carrier but the dangerous trunking system was still practised by smaller boats. These trawlers are undergoing repair and inspection in the dry dock at Grimsby about 1903.*

52. *King's Lynn boasted several shipbuilding yards like this at the turn of the century. It was customary for the work to be done out of doors and for the stock to be erected on public quays. In these circumstances a tonnage duty was paid to the Corporation. Note the large tree trunks on the highway. They have just been unloaded from the drugs.*

53. *The entire complement of twenty men pose for the photographer with the Yarmouth lifeboat 'Hugh Taylor'. She was a pulling and sailing boat built in the usual Norfolk and Suffolk design for the Royal National Lifeboat Institution. She was taken out of service at the outbreak of the First World War in 1914 and as a result of the reduction in stations made possible by the introduction of motor lifeboats she was never replaced.*

54. *The crew of the Caister lifeboat 'Beauchamp', 'perhaps the finest lifeboat crew the world has ever seen', was wiped out on the night of 4th November 1901. In terrible conditions she went to the aid of the Lowestoft smack 'Buttercup', but largely as a result of an accident to the mizzen sheet she capsized in the surf.*

55. *In 1814 a ship's figurehead, a wooden dolly, was placed on Custom House Quay, North Shields. It became the tradition for the notoriously superstitious sailors of the time to cut pieces off it as good luck tokens before sailing. It was not long before the dolly had been whittled away. Fortunately she and her successors have always been replaced. This, the fourth wooden dolly, was carved by Sarah Spence and placed on Custom House Quay, or Wooden Dolly Quay, as it was invariably called in 1902. The fifth figure, carved in 1958, still stands in Northumberland Square, North Shields.*

56. *This fine old wooden barquentine 'Hilda of Faversham' pictured at Blyth in about 1904 alongside a large North American fore and aft schooner, was built at Appledore, Devon, by Alfred Cook in 1879. She was 233 tons register and her twelve-foot draught was a handicap to her as a coaster. She spent most of her life in the Cornish china clay trade but she was sunk in 1930 when carrying coal from Blyth to St Austell. She was cut in two by the trawler 'Kudos' fifteen miles from Hartlepool and went down in two minutes.*

57. (Left) *Most of the Scottish drifters fishing for herring off the East Coast were rigged with a dipping lug foresail and a standing lug mizzen sheeted to a bumkin. The Zulu pictured here has a stern post raked aft from the keel and is derived from the Skaffie, another vessel from the east coast of Scotland which had both raking stem and stern posts. The heavy foremast is lowered when the boat rides to her nets but it is neither weighted nor pivoted and is stepped by means of a steam capstan.*

58. (Right) *This is the training ship 'Wellesley' which was such a familiar feature of the Tyne from 1868, when she was first moored there, until she was gutted by fire in 1914. Built in 1844 and originally named 'Boscawen', she and ships like her ensured the continuing dominance of British sea power once the Napoleonic Wars were over. Thousands of officers and men learned their trades aboard this ship — one of the last of the wooden walls of England.*

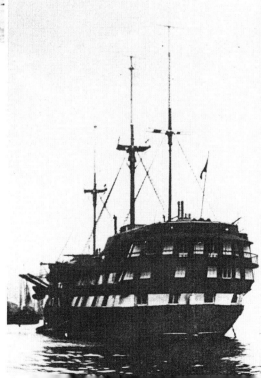

59. *This netting shed was the place of work for all the women in this photograph taken in the Norfolk village of Winterton about 1905. They were beatsters employed in making and mending the nets which their fishermen husbands were to use at sea. The men's outer clothing, or 'slops' as they were called, were dyed in the small rectangular building to the left. It was called the tanning copper and was chiefly used for treating the nets.*

60. (Top right) *These fishermen, photographed in August 1904, harvested the crabs and lobsters for which Cromer and Sheringham are famous. The rocky sea bed was a natural habitat but the fishermen took no chances and when they returned to Sheringham in the spring, after crabbing off the Yorkshire coast, they brought back with them a supply of live crabs to replenish the local stock. They also agreed not to bring ashore any crab smaller than four-and-a-half inches and a fine of one pound was levied on defaulters. The crab pot began to replace the older hoop net in the nineteenth century.*

61. (Lower right) *This crab boat, photographed in Sheringham about 1904, is typical of those made there from 1820. Some sixteen feet long, they were double-ended, clinker-built and usually of oak. Some, especially if used for whelking, were of larch. They had no gunwale and neither thole pins nor rowlocks. Instead three ports were cut in the topmost strake on either side. When the boat was carried up the beach an oar was passed through these ports and used as handles. The stem and stern posts were rounded, there were no floorboards and the sail used was a dipping lug.*

62. *'Resolution' was one of those magnificent battleships built by Palmers on Tyneside in 1893. Like the other six ships in the Royal Sovereign class she was 380 feet long and had a displacement of 14,100 tons. She cost £900,000 and carried a complement of 712 men. This photograph can be dated accurately, for the striking topmast was added after 1903 and the gaff removed in February 1905. Her main armament consisted of four thirteen-inch and ten six-inch guns. She steamed at fifteen knots, but at this speed consumed ten tons of coal every hour.*

63. *The Tyne is not usually associated with luggers fishing for herring but in 1872, about thirty years before this picture was taken, 489 fishing boats of under fifteen tons were registered in North Shields and 44 at South Shields. Details of fishing vessels are recorded in special registers maintained by county administrations. The marking usually consists of the first and last letters in the name of the town of registration: e.g. GY for Grimsby, WY for Whitby, followed by a numeral. Most European nations register their fishing vessels in the same way.*

64. *The black-sailed trader, to give the wherry its common name, was a familiar sight on the rivers and broads of Norfolk and Suffolk. She carried cargo about the country economically and safely from around 1775. No wherry trades now but 'Albion' is preserved by the Norfolk Wherry Trust. The wherry's most notable feature was its large gaff sail, free at the foot. It had a shallow draught and its supporters maintained that it could sail over a green field provided there had been a heavy dew.*

65. (Below) *Many of the earliest steamboats were designed to tow barges on canals and rivers but they were pressed into service from time to time to assist sailormen who had lost the wind. The first steam paddle tugs, far removed from their powerful successors pictured here about 1906, appeared on the Tyne in 1822. They were particularly adept in handling the colliers and their use spread to the Thames in 1832.*

66. *Most of the East Coast ports are strongly tidal and in some places even the smallest vessels have difficulty in making harbour at certain states of the tide. Some ports dry out completely and vessels engaged in the coasting trade must therefore not only be shallow-draughted but be designed to lie on the sea bed without damaging themselves. This snow at anchor and lying on the mud at King's Lynn in 1906 has unloaded her cargo into the barge alongside and the four men have ferried it to the quayside.*

67. (Above) *These fishing boats, some of them fifies from Scotland, with their huge dipping lugsails caused quite a traffic jam at the mouth of the Yare about 1906 but a few years later they were all superseded by the ubiquitous steam drifter. Luggers of this type were originally rigged with three masts but by 1874 the mainmast was dispensed with because it impeded fishing.*
Luggers became popular on the East Coast soon after 1800 and by 1850 had replaced in their entirety the old herring busses with their giant square-rigged sail amidships.

68. (Above) *It was unusual to see a caulker at work on Scarborough beach as late as 1908. The yawl 'Good Design' is carvel-built; that is to say that the planks of her side are evenly laid one upon the other and do not overlap like those of a clinker-built vessel. In carvel-built vessels the seams between the planks are stuffed with oakum and then painted over with hot pitch to make them water-tight. The caulker was never seen without his tool box for it served as a seat, but this tradesman prefers a fish box!*

69. (Left) *The launching of the battleship 'Lord Nelson' from Palmer's yard on the Tyne was on 4th September 1906. She was more heavily protected than her predecessors and the first to have solid bulkheads. The last British battleship fitted with a mixed main armament, consisting of four twelve-inch and ten 9.2-inch guns, she had no bridges and was also the last of our battleships to have reciprocating engines. She was the flagship of the channel fleet and took part in the shelling of Chanack in the Dardanelles campaign of 1915. She was sold in 1920.*

70. *The expertise of the Tyne shipyards in the building of warships was frequently recognised by foreign governments. The Brazilian cruiser 'Rio Grande Do Sul' has just been launched from the Elswick yard on 20th April 1909. She was fitted with Parsons turbines, Yarrow boilers and Vickers machinery. She carried ten 4.7-inch guns, six three-pounders and two torpedo tubes above water. Her complement was 320 men and she could steam for 1,400 miles at 23 knots.*

71. *Turret ships like 'Pearlmoor', seen here discharging timber at Hull in 1908, are vessels without sheer. That is to say there is no vertical curve in the ship's deckline between bow and stern. The rounded turret deck is the top of the hull proper and above this a narrow structure runs fore and aft. All are now obsolete. Ships built to this design had great longitudinal strength.*

72. *Around 1912 'King Coal', a vessel of 300 feet in length and carrying a load of 1,000 tons of coal, was a familiar sight. She provided a full bunkering for the early steam drifters, each of which burned between five and ten tons of coal every week. She was first towed to the Shetlands and as the herring and the drifters moved south she followed in their wake. It was customary for the men who did the bunkering to live aboard and it was not unusual for them to be away for three or four months at a time.*

73. *Holidaymakers at Great Yarmouth setting out in the summer of 1910 for a trip in the 'King Edward VII' little realised that in the winter she reverted to her usual role of paddle tug. On the night of Friday 21st October she pulled off the Caister lifeboat under the command of 'Spratt' Haylett to go to the aid of a ship aground on Scroby Sands.*

74. *An Edwardian blood in a striped blazer, young men in tight-fitting caps and their elders in fashionable bowlers, accompanied by their ladies, all prepare to enjoy a sail in the 'James Amis'. These beach boats resembled the older beach yawls although for ease of handling they were often rigged cutter fashion. With their green gunwales, white painted hulls and sails bellying in the breeze they made an attractive spectacle.*

75. *(Right) The Humber keel, this is 'Sunbeam' of Stainforth photographed on the Trent in 1910, was essentially a vessel designed for the carrying of cargo on inland waterways. It was normally of oak and carvel-built. The mast was usually stepped in a tabernacle just forward of amidships and could easily be lowered when shooting bridges. Its large square sail was often augmented by a square topsail set on a yard almost as long as the mainyard. The keel could be sailed close to the wind and the modern introduction of wires and hand winches enabled her to be managed by one man.*

76. *The leeboard, clearly visible on the spritsail barge 'Valdora' at Great Yarmouth, was lowered until it projected beneath the vessel's bottom when she was sailed closehauled. It then acted as a keel and prevented her from being driven to leeward. She was fifty-six tons register and built in 1904 by Shrubsall for Hammond. Many smaller barges had their spritmizzens sheeted to the end of the rudder blade so that the sail, turning with the rudder, became a rudder in the air. This, with the foresail aback, enabled the barge to be turned when she had no leeway.*

Winterton Lighthouse

77. (Above) *Before 1911 only the skipper and mate of a trawler were paid by results. The basic rate for the rest of the crew ranged from forty-six shillings for engineers to one pound per week for deck hands. The Grimsby owners, because of rising costs, then tried to introduce a share element into everybody's pay. This was fiercely resisted by the engineers and, as pictured here, the entire fleet was laid up for fourteen weeks while the dispute lasted. After arbitration the men conceded the point and were partly paid on the share system. This revolutionised the wage structure of the industry.*

78. (Left) *Before 1820 the mariner had very few ways of differentiating between lighthouses; and eighty-five per cent of the world's lighthouses showed fixed lights. Of these, the navigators preferred a light obtained from a brightly burning coal fire like that at Winterton between 1678 and 1746. Although such fires had a power of less than one hundred candles they caused no confusion with ships' navigation lights and from other lights ashore. This light, transferred to Trinity House in 1836, was in use in 1910, the probable date of this photograph, but has now been converted into a private dwelling.*

79. (Above) *Colchester, renowned for its oyster fisheries, has always had a coasting trade. Here at Hythe Quay about 1912 Thames barges are waiting to load grain. The oyster smack was one of the last remaining fishing vessels to be cutter rigged. The weight of the spars aloft, the intricate nature of the rigging and the impossibility of lowering the mast on deck proved too much of a handicap in most waters. In the narrow channels of the Essex estuaries her handiness and speed more than compensated for these disadvantages.*

80. (Left) *The mission ship 'Euston', with sails in tatters after the gales of 1911, has cause to be proud of her service. The mission was introduced in 1881 by E. J. Mather to ease the seamen's lot and prevent them from being 'rooked' by vessels cruising among the fleets selling raw liquor. Enticed aboard by the lure of cheap tobacco they were persuaded to buy drink. The mission boats carried medical supplies, books and comforts. The men at first greeted them with derision but, finding that religion was not thrust down their throats, came to bless them.*

81. (Top right) *Each autumn for well over a hundred years Scots fishergirls followed the herring down the East Coast. They cleaned, salted and packed the catch which their husbands and sweethearts harvested on the Smith's Knoll and other fishing grounds of the North Sea. They usually worked for the same merchant year after year and their daughters, when they were old enough, followed the same ill-rewarded occupation.*

82. (Lower right) *The coaster 'Gwendolynne Birch' of Hull, photographed in King's Lynn about 1913, is typical of most of the steamers in the East Coast cargo-carrying trade. They are sturdily built to face up to the bad weather continually encountered in the North Sea. It is important that they can lie on the ground without straining themselves. All the machinery is in the after part of the ship and this ensures that she has long unencumbered holds with big hatches to facilitate unloading. Most ships of this type have raised quarter decks and measure less than 200 feet in length.*

83. (Below) *The years from 1900 to 1919 were the hey-day for East Coast herring fishing. In 1913 nearly two and a half million hundredweights of fish were caught by 1,163 boats. Here are some of the barrels of salted and cured herring waiting to be exported to Russia and the Mediterranean countries. These markets were lost as a result of the First World War and the industry has never completely recovered.*

84. (Above) *Blyth is associated with brigs and sea-going colliers but before the development of the coal trade in the seventeenth century it was engaged primarily in the export of salt to London. Timber has always been an important import but the antiquated unloading equipment pictured here about 1920 was replaced long ago by modern mobile cranes, fork-lift trucks, grain conveyors and all the modern equipment found in an efficient port. The rolling stock in the foreground belongs to the Blyth Harbour Commission, founded in 1882, which created the modern port.*

85. (Right) *The photograph of this large sailing vessel, being towed into port with her deck cargo clearly visible, dates from about 1920; for ships of this sort, engaged primarily in the grain and timber trade, survived longer than most sailormen. She is a three-masted barque, being square rigged on the fore and main masts and fore and aft rigged on the mizzen. Barques with four or even five masts were common at one time and in these ships too all masts were square rigged with the exception of the aftermost one which was again rigged fore and aft.*

86. (Left) *This wooden barquentine 'Estonia' from Mariehamn on Aland Island in Finland photographed in port in 1921 is one of the smallest units, being 475 tons gross, in the Erikson fleet. Ships of this type were used almost exclusively in the coasting trade but a few barquentines, such as the famous French vessel 'Terre Neuva', were designed as ocean-going ships.*

87. (Right) *'Pet', pictured here at the bar at Yarmouth harbour in the early 1920s, is passing a steamer with no wheelhouse. 'Pet' is a typical Lowestoft trawler, whose numbers had been steadily declining since that day in November 1877 when the tug 'Messenger', as a result of economic expediency, became the first steam vessel to successfully haul a trawl. The last sailing drifter disappeared during the First World War but even as late as 1939 Lowestoft possessed a small fleet of sailing trawlers.*

88. *For hundreds of years timber from the Baltic has been one of the staple cargoes of the East Coast ports. Although many ordinary tramp steamers carried wood a special type like 'Jessie', pictured here about 1922, were specially developed for the trade. To enable her to take the large deck load she has long clear well decks with derricks not only at bow and stern but also amidships. The coal-burning timber ships of this sort were between one thousand and two thousand tons but they are a rare sight nowadays having been superseded by faster and more economical vessels.*

89. *The steam tug 'Richard Lee Barber' is having difficulty in turning this unladen cargo vessel in the river Yare about 1955. All the earliest steam driven cargo ships were completely flush-decked like this. They had the same long continuous deck running from bow to stern. There were the usual erections around the funnel and engine room skylight. The spar-decked ship with its more elaborate erections amidships was a natural development but ships of this type were far less popular than the three island type of cargo carrying ships.*

90. *In 1926 the Lowestoft steam drifter 'Justifier' seemed the acme of sophistication especially when compared with the fishing smack in the background. Yet smacks such as this fished out of Lowestoft until the outbreak of the Second World War and now both types of vessel are obsolete. The only steam drifter known to be in existence is 'Lydia Eva', built in Lynn for H. J. Eastick of Yarmouth and now owned by the Maritime Trust.*

91. *Despite her large sail area, this five-masted Vinnen two-top sail schooner was fitted with auxiliary power when she was photographed at King's Lynn on 21st October 1923. She is 'Susanne Vinnen' of 1,859 tons register and she has just arrived from Rosario with a cargo of maize.*

92. *A steam drifter leaving harbour in a north-easterly wind. A strong ebb of about three to four knots and a fresh on-shore wind have combined to cause heavy seas at the bar to swamp this vessel.*

93. *By the time the 'Sir William Archibald' came into service the Mission to Deep Sea Fishermen had obtained permission to carry tobacco free of duty. The smacksmen now had no need to go aboard foreign vessels for cheap tobacco and so the fleet was left in peace. 'Sir William Archibald', like all mission smacks, was fitted with a wheel instead of a tiller, was fifty-six tons register and built as recently as 1927.*

94. *In a modern lightship the lantern is mounted on a hollow steel tower and the crew can tend it completely protected from the weather. With engines fitted below to provide the motive power for dynamo and foghorn it is a miniature lighthouse. How different things were on this Humber lightship in 1928. Then the mast passed through the lantern which is shown being lowered to the deck. Now most of the manned light vessels have been replaced with fixed lights built on platforms like those in the North Sea Gas enterprise. One such light marks the Inner Dowsing fifteen miles off Skegness.*

95. *Throughout the 1920s and 30s the home drifter fleets were augmented by those of other European nations with the inevitable result that the North Sea was gradually denuded of herring. Nevertheless some ships like the 'Naviedale' were still engaged in the export of herring until the outbreak of the Second World War. She is pictured here coming into Yarmouth with a load of empty barrels. These will be packed with herrings put between layers of salt and exported, on this occasion, to the Low Countries.*

96. *Trinity House maintains a fleet of tenders to carry provisions, spares and supplies to the lighthouses. They also take out the relief crews and service the buoys and navigation marks on their round. 'Warden', a coal-burning ship, was typical of the breed. Built in 1929, she was in her prime capable of a speed in excess of ten knots. Here we see her in 1930 about to cast-off and loaded with newly painted buoys, the people alongside giving a fair indication of their size. Like coal-burners everywhere she became too expensive to run and was taken out of service in 1959.*

97. (Above) *This strange vessel is the cable ship 'Alert' about 1930. Her job is the laying and repair of submarine cables. To do this she has sheaves both at the stern and the bow to facilitate the taking in and paying out of the cable, tasks performed by powerful windlasses. Specially designed grapnels are fitted in order to pick up the cable from the sea bed. The large hold is required for storing the many buoys needed on the job. She is also fitted with large circular tanks which contain the cable coiled round central cones.*

98. (Right) *This suction dredger is indeed a weird vessel but familiar enough in the Wash and at Lowestoft where she was photographed about 1930. Specially designed for working in sand or soft mud she resembled a giant floating vacum cleaner. The nozzles, seen clearly in the photograph, are at the ends of large pipes and they are lowered onto the sea bed. The powerful centrifugal pumps in the hull then suck up the mud. Some vessels intended for service in other parts of the country and having to cope with firm clay are often fitted with rotating cutters on the nozzles.*

99. *The sprit, that enormous spar which runs from the foot of the mast and diagonally across the mainsail to support it at the peak, can be clearly seen in this photograph of the coasting barge 'Will Everard'. Her bowsprit too has been lifted to a near vertical position, a normal procedure in harbour. She was ninety-seven feet long, twenty-three feet in the beam and carried 5,000 square feet of sail exclusive of balloon canvas. Her working livery was grey hull with pink bottom and black rails with a gold sheer line.*

100. *Tankers like the 'B.P. Supervisor' are employed in the coastal distribution of oil and petroleum from the big depots to the smaller ones scattered around the country. Between 1924 and 1930 the growing demand for tanker tonnage led to a simpler type of construction. In consequence the building of tankers became a speciality of the North East and during those years 159 ships representing a million tons were built there. This was one-third of the world's total output of tankers.*

101. *The first light vessel to be placed on station off the East Coast was that at the Dudgeon in 1736. Of course the sandy shores of the East Coast, unlike the rocky south and west, provided a poor foundation for lighthouses and it was natural enough that lightships should therefore proliferate. By the end of the nineteenth century there were no fewer than fourteen lightships marking potential danger spots between Harwich and King's Lynn. They were serviced by a series of supply ships such as the Trinity House vessel, 'Vestal', which was in commission from 1898 to 1928.*

102. *This self-propelling hopper, photographed in 1935 whilst waiting to take up station alongside the dredger, is designed to deposit the soil dredged up from the East Coast harbours onto the recognised dumping grounds well out in the North Sea. Many of these ships are two hundred feet long and have a soil carrying capacity of about a thousand tons. They are fitted with bottom doors which release the soil through the bottom of the ship.*

103. (Right) *'Cambria', pictured here at Yarmouth in 1959, was the last coasting barge to be worked entirely under sail. She is mulie rigged in that she has a sprit mainsail and a ketch mizzen carrying a gaff and a boom placed forward of the wheel. Her total sail area is 5,000 square feet. She was built at Greenhithe in 1906 for £1,895 and she was still sailing profitably as recently as 1971. Then she was acquired for the nation by the Maritime Trust from Bob Roberts, her last owner and skipper.*

104. *Were it not for the small gun on the forecastle one could be forgiven for thinking that this is a common or garden trawler. She is in fact a class 5 Fishery Patrol vessel, photographed in Lowestoft in the early 1930s. She has twin screws and is very much faster than she looks. She has a very shallow draught. The motor boat usually carried forward is concealed by the bulwarks.*

BIBLIOGRAPHY

Black Sailed Traders; R. Clark; Putnam, 1961.
British Fishing Boats and Coastal Craft; E.W.White; HMSO, 1950.
Collier Brigs and their Sailors; Sir Walter Runciman; Conway Maritime Press, 1971.
Down Tops'l; H. Benham; Harrap, 1971.
East Coast Passage; C. Clarke; Longmans, 1971.
Historic Ships ; M. K. Stammers; Shire, 1987.
Inshore Craft of Britain; E. J. March; David & Charles, 1970.
Jane's Fighting Ships; various editors; Samson Low, various.
Lore of Ships; T. Trychare; Heinemann, 1964.
Sailing Barges; F. G. C. Carr; Peter Davies, 1951.
Sailing Drifters; E. J. March; David & Charles, 1969.
Sailing Trawlers; E. J. March; David & Charles, 1970.
Sails through the Centuries; San Svenson; Macmillan, n.d.
Ships and Shipping; M. D. Palmer; Batsford, 1971.
Ships, Boats and Craft; S. E. Beck; Jenkins, 1942.
West Coast Shipping; M. K. Stammers; Shire, 1989.
Wherries and Waterways; R. W. Maltster; Dalton, 1971.

Photographic Acknowledgements
The figures refer to plate numbers
Mr Brian Ollington: Cover.
Mr A. W. Yallop: 16, 34, 36, 46, 74, 76, 81, 92
Mr C. R. Temple: 8, 13, 17, 38, 57, 71, 85, 86, 87, 88, 89, 90, 94, 95, 96, 97, 98, 99, 100, 103, 104
Mrs B. George: 59
Mrs M. Woodhouse: 42, 78
Mr S. Storey: 80
Mr J. Johnson: 24, 25, 40, 50, 53
Mr C. Briggs: 83, 93,
Scarborough Public Library: 6, 15, 19, 22, 26, 35, 68
Teesside Public Libraries: 1, 3, 5, 9
Tynemouth County Borough Libraries: 23, 32, 44, 55, 58
King's Lynn Public Libraries: 27, 33, 49, 52, 66, 82, 91
Newcastle-on-Tyne City Libraries: 45, 62, 63, 65, 69, 70
Ipswich and E. Suffolk Record Office: 39
Grimsby Public Libraries: 51, 77
Ipswich Public Libraries: 18, 31
Blyth Public Library: 10, 56, 84
Colchester Public Library: 79
Humber Keel and Sloop Preservation Society: 75
Great Yarmouth Public Libraries: 2, 11, 12, 20, 37, 43, 47, 48, 60, 61, 64, 72, 102
Maritime Museum for East Anglia: 4, 7, 14, 28, 30, 41, 54, 67,
Trinity House: 101
M. A. Hedges: 21, 29, 72

Index

A paddle tug passing the North Pier on the river Wear c. 1900.